SPORTS GREAT DENNIS RODMAN

— *Sports Great Books* —

BASEBALL

Sports Great Jim Abbott
0-89490-395-0/ Savage

Sports Great Bobby Bonilla
0-89490-417-5/ Knapp

Sports Great Ken Griffey, Jr.
0-7660-1266-2/ Savage

Sports Great Orel Hershiser
0-89490-389-6/ Knapp

Sports Great Bo Jackson
0-89490-281-4/ Knapp

Sports Great Greg Maddux
0-89490-873-1/ Thornley

Sports Great Kirby Puckett
0-89490-392-6/ Aaseng

Sports Great Cal Ripken, Jr.
0-89490-387-X/ Macnow

Sports Great Nolan Ryan
0-89490-394-2/ Lace

Sports Great Darryl Strawberry
0-89490-291-1/ Torres & Sullivan

Sports Great Frank Thomas
0-7660-1269-7/ Deane

BASKETBALL

**Sports Great Charles Barkley
(Revised Edition)**
0-7660-1004-X/ Macnow

Sports Great Larry Bird
0-89490-368-3/ Kavanagh

Sports Great Kobe Bryant
0-7660-1264-6/ Macnow

Sports Great Muggsy Bogues
0-89490-876-6/ Rekela

Sports Great Patrick Ewing
0-89490-369-1/ Kavanagh

Sports Great Kevin Garnett
0-7660-1263-8/ Macnow

Sports Great Anfernee Hardaway
0-89490-758-1/ Rekela

Sports Great Juwan Howard
0-7660-1065-1/ Savage

**Sports Great Magic Johnson
(Revised and Expanded)**
0-89490-348-9/ Haskins

**Sports Great Michael Jordan
(Revised Edition)**
0-89490-978-9/ Aaseng

Sports Great Jason Kidd
0-7660-1001-5/ Torres

Sports Great Karl Malone
0-89490-599-6/ Savage

Sports Great Reggie Miller
0-89490-874-X/ Thornley

Sports Great Alonzo Mourning
0-89490-875-8/ Fortunato

Sports Great Dikembe Mutombo
0-7660-1267-0/ Torres

**Sports Great Shaquille O'Neal
(Revised Edition)**
0-7660-1003-1/ Sullivan

Sports Great Scottie Pippen
0-89490-755-7/ Bjarkman

Sports Great Mitch Richmond
0-7660-1070-8/ Grody

**Sports Great David Robinson
(Revised Edition)**
0-7660-1077-5/ Aaseng

Sports Great Dennis Rodman
0-89490-759-X/ Thornley

Sports Great John Stockton
0-89490-598-8/ Aaseng

Sports Great Isiah Thomas
0-89490-374-8/ Knapp

Sports Great Chris Webber
0-7660-1069-4/ Macnow

Sports Great Dominique Wilkins
0-89490-754-9/ Bjarkman

FOOTBALL

Sports Great Troy Aikman
0-89490-593-7/ Macnow

Sports Great Jerome Bettis
0-89490-872-3/ Majewski

Sports Great John Elway
0-89490-282-2/ Fox

Sports Great Brett Favre
0-7660-1000-7/ Savage

Sports Great Jim Kelly
0-89490-670-4/ Harrington

Sports Great Joe Montana
0-89490-371-3/ Kavanagh

Sports Great Jerry Rice
0-89490-419-1/ Dickey

**Sports Great Barry Sanders
(Revised Edition)**
0-7660-1067-8/ Knapp

Sports Great Deion Sanders
0-7660-1068-6/ Macnow

Sports Great Emmitt Smith
0-7660-1002-3/ Grabowski

Sports Great Herschel Walker
0-89490-207-5/ Benagh

OTHER

Sports Great Michael Chang
0-7660-1223-9/ Ditchfield

Sports Great Oscar De La Hoya
0-7660-1066-X/ Torres

Sports Great Steffi Graf
0-89490-597-X/ Knapp

Sports Great Wayne Gretzky
0-89490-757-3/ Rappoport

Sports Great Mario Lemieux
0-89490-596-1/ Knapp

Sports Great Eric Lindros
0-89490-871-5/ Rappoport

Sports Great Pete Sampras
0-89490-756-5/ Sherrow

SPORTS GREAT
DENNIS
RODMAN

Stew Thornley

— Sports Great Books —

Enslow Publishers, Inc.

40 Industrial Road   PO Box 38
Box 398   Aldershot
Berkeley Heights, NJ   07922   Hants GU12 6BP
USA   UK

http://www.enslow.com

Library of Congress Cataloging-in-Publication Data

Thornley, Stew.
   Sports great Dennis Rodman / Stew Thornley.
   p. cm. — (Sports great books)
   Includes index.
   ISBN 0-89490-759-X
   1. Rodman, Dennis, 1961– —Juvenile literature. 2. Basketball players—United
States—Biography—Juvenile literature. I. Title. II. Series.
GV884.R618T47   1996
796.323'092—dc20
[B]   95-9229
                                                    CIP
                                                    AC

Printed in the United States of America

10 9 8 7 6 5

To Our Readers:
All Internet addresses in this book were active and appropriate when we went to press. Any
comments or suggestions can be sent by e-mail to Comments@enslow.com or to the address
on the back cover.

Illustration Credits: Brian Drake, Rim Light Photography Inc., pp. 9, 13, 50, 52,
55, 57, 59; Courtesy of Shirley Rodman, pp. 17, 19, 21, 25, 27, 31, 44; NBA
Photos, Allen Einstein, p. 40; NBA Photos, Nathaniel S. Butler, p. 38.

Cover Photo: Robert Mora/NBA Photos

Contents

Chapter 1

Basketball highlight films usually show the ball going through the basket. Rarely do they show shots that miss, clanging off the rim and falling away. But it is at that point that Dennis Rodman goes to work.

Rebounding is one of the most important tasks on a basketball court, but it is an often-overlooked skill. Dennis Rodman is one of the best in the business in grabbing missed shots—keeping alive rallies for his team and making sure opponents don't get second chances at baskets.

By the middle of the 1992–93 season, Rodman led the National Basketball Association (NBA) with more than 17 rebounds per game. He had led the league in rebounding in 1991 and 1992 with totals not seen in the league for more than twenty years.

Even so, when the NBA All-Star game was played at the Target Center in Minnesota in 1994, Dennis Rodman was not on the team. The fans and coaches had picked other, more high-profile, players to represent the Eastern and Western Conference squads.

Dennis Rodman found himself at the Target Center, but eight days after the All-Star game was played. His team, the San Antonio Spurs, was looking for its thirteenth-straight win as it took on the Minnesota Timberwolves. Once again, the spotlight was elsewhere.

Rodman's teammate, superstar center David Robinson, got off to a great start, scoring 18 points in the first quarter. Even with Robinson pouring in points, the Spurs were up by only one point at halftime.

Through it all, Rodman was steadily grabbing rebounds. He cut inside following a missed Minnesota shot and took one away from Timberwolves' center Mike Brown. At the other end of the court, he kept the ball alive for the Spurs after they missed a shot. As Rodman piled up the rebounds and Robinson added to his point total, the Spurs opened up a comfortable lead in the third quarter.

Dennis Rodman made sure the Timberwolves couldn't get back into the game in the final period. As a shot from J.R. Rider fell short off the rim for Minnesota, Rodman jumped high to grab it away from Marlon Maxey. A missed shot by Doug West disappeared into Rodman's arms.

San Antonio went on to win the game by 25 points. The attention after the game was on David Robinson, who scored 50 points. Overlooked was the fact that Dennis Rodman had 20 rebounds, another benchmark of excellence. It was the eighth time during the Spurs' thirteen-game winning streak that Rodman had at least 20 rebounds.

Fans and the media were more dazzled by high point totals, and Robinson, not Rodman, was the subject of postgame interviews. But Robinson was not about to forget the contributions of Dennis Rodman, who was in his first year with the Spurs. Robinson pointed out the great game Rodman also had and cited Rodman's value to the team the entire

Rodman wore this mask during most of the Spurs' thirteen-game winning streak in order to protect an injury he had suffered.

season. Those who play with and against Dennis Rodman know exactly how much he does for his team.

And it's not just rebounding, either. Dennis Rodman is also one of the best defensive players in the game. Twice in his career, he's been named the NBA Defensive Player of the Year, and he has been a member of the league's All-Defensive team for five consecutive years.

It's been his job to guard the top scorers on the other teams—players like Michael Jordan, Larry Bird, and Magic Johnson. Although some people would rather not have such a job, Rodman welcomes it. In fact, he feels hurt if he isn't assigned to the opponent's best scorer.

Defensive giants in the league make their contributions by blocking shots. Fans love this kind of "in-your-face" action.

But Rodman doesn't focus on flashy defensive play. He plays defense by harassing the other scorers up and down the court, not just when they're shooting. Sometimes he forces them into situations in which they can be double-teamed. He may also cause them to turn over the ball or commit an offensive foul.

An assistant coach with the Detroit Pistons, where Dennis Rodman played before coming to the Spurs, once said, "Only two players in NBA history can influence a game to this extent by playing defense: Bill Russell and Dennis Rodman."

Bill Russell is considered by some to be the best defensive player ever. To be mentioned in the same sentence with him, as Dennis Rodman was, is a great honor.

Perhaps one of Rodman's greatest skills is not just knowing his strengths but recognizing his limitations. One of his limitations is scoring. He doesn't try—for that matter, some say he doesn't even want—to score points in large numbers.

Rodman would rather stop others from scoring and grab missed shots to give his teammates the chance to score.

Chuck Daly, his coach with the Detroit Pistons, said, "He'll win you six to ten games a year without even scoring."

Daly added that he was delighted to have a player like Rodman on his team. "I love him," said Daly. "As a coach, you go to the wall for a player like that." Not all of Rodman's future coaches, however, would express the same feelings.

Although he plays the game in a nonflashy way, it doesn't mean that Dennis Rodman doesn't stand out. He has often drawn attention to himself, sometimes when he didn't even intend to do so.

His rookie season in the NBA ended with a loss in the playoffs to the Boston Celtics, who were led by Larry Bird. Afterward a frustrated Rodman said that Bird was overrated.

His remarks caused a great deal of controversy. Rodman eventually apologized for his outburst, although he wasn't sure that his comments were incorrect.

Rodman also stands out on the court with his hair, which he changes the color of frequently. Rodman's body is also covered with tattoos. These are especially noticeable, since basketball uniforms do little to cover a player's body.

Dennis Rodman has always been known for his hustle on the court. Even that, Rodman found, could bring trouble. He once dove for a loose ball and sailed into the crowd, where he crashed into a spectator, injuring her. His actions were ruled reckless and Rodman had to pay damages.

Reckless is certainly a term that can also extend to Dennis Rodman's life off the basketball court. When he's hurting, experiencing tough times, he can do things that leave people shaking their heads and wondering about him.

Life for Dennis Rodman has never been easy. Coming from a broken home, he had little self-esteem. He was a skinny kid who spent a lot of time playing pinball. Because of the twisting he did while trying to direct the pinball, he became known as "Worm," a nickname that is still with him.

But his life lacked purpose and direction before he found success in basketball, a game he didn't really begin playing until he was twenty.

Although the word rebound has meaning to Rodman on the court, it may be more important to his life off it. Rebounding, or bouncing back from tough times, is something he has had to do more than once.

He was helped by an Oklahoma family, who virtually "adopted" him while he was in college. He developed a friendship with a member of that family who was also dealing with emotional scars, and the two helped each other along.

Dennis Rodman's story is an amazing one of dealing with and overcoming emotional challenges that exist for him to this day. Although he has sometimes caused concern to the teams for whom he has played, none could ever deny the effort Dennis puts in as a player. "I love pain," Dennis Rodman once said. "It makes me feel like I'm accomplishing something." Rodman believes in working for what he gets, even to the point of avoiding elevators because he feels guilty about traveling up or down a floor with no effort.

But in addition to physical effort and hustle, Dennis Rodman works hard at getting to know the game. He spends a great deal of time studying the opposing players, getting to know their strengths and weaknesses.

This preparation helps him in many ways, including rebounding. "When the ball is two feet out of a shooter's hand, Rodman has the judgment to know if it's going to be short, long left, short right, whatever," says San Antonio vice president Bob Bass. "He gets the best jump on the ball in the NBA."

As the Blazers try to prevent him from doing what he does best, Rodman goes up for the rebound.

Rodman himself sums up his success rebounding in simpler terms. "How do you dig a 50-foot hole?" he asks. "You dig. How do I get a rebound? I go get the basketball."

His thoughts on playing defense are just as simple: "Defense is about knowing what a player can do and can't do—and then making him do what he can't."

Chapter 2

Shirley and Phil Rodman were married for only a few years. There were a lot of problems between them. Finally, Shirley and Phil Rodman split up. By this time, they had three children together.

The oldest, Dennis, was born May 13, 1961, in Trenton, New Jersey, where his father was stationed in the United States Air Force. The Rodmans then had two daughters, Debra and Kim, before Shirley finally packed up her belongings—and her kids—and moved back to her home in Dallas.

The Rodmans had to struggle. Shirley Rodman sometimes had four jobs at one time to earn enough to support the family by herself. She not only taught school, she brought in her own students as she drove the school bus in the morning. She also taught voice and played the piano and organ in church on Sundays, and held down a job in a department store on weeknights. The money she earned from her jobs to buy food and clothes for her kids was important. But it wasn't enough. Shirley Rodman somehow found time between jobs to spend time with her son and daughters, instilling values in them.

Dennis especially missed having a father and needed more attention than his sisters. Shirley Rodman thinks it was stress her son felt from not having a dad that resulted in allergy attacks and his face breaking out in open sores. Years later, Shirley Rodman had second thoughts about how she handled the family situation. She thinks Dennis may have been better able to cope with it if she had discussed the split-up with him. She said:

> He didn't have a father around, but it wasn't like he grew up in a cruel lifestyle. He didn't grow up in a ghetto or anything like that. He was very shy and introverted and didn't mingle well with others. I think he just always had trouble finding himself—figuring out who he was.

Dennis's sisters, on the other hand, appeared much more well adjusted, better able to handle the adversity of a broken home. Even though they were younger, Debra and Kim watched over Dennis.

Dennis matured slowly—both physically and emotionally. As his sisters sprouted up and became better at sports, Dennis lagged behind and felt even more awkward.

Although he didn't play on any organized teams in his early years, Dennis enjoyed playing sports. When his mother worked evenings, she left the kids at a recreation center where they would play basketball. "Dennis just loved playing with his sisters," Shirley Rodman remembers, "but he never had any confidence."

Dennis Rodman tried out for the football team, when he was in tenth grade at South Oak Cliff High School. He could run well and won a sprinting trial. Even so, he was passed up for a spot on the squad because the coaches thought he was too small.

He did make the school's basketball team, but did little more than warm the bench. He was lacking in both size (he was only five-foot-nine when he graduated from high school)

As a teenager, Dennis Rodman enjoyed playing sports. He would play basketball at the local recreation center.

and skills. "I couldn't even make a layup right," he later said. After half a season, he quit the team.

He had no close friends through high school and was seen as a loner. Much of his free time was spent at home, by himself, or tagging along with his sisters Debra and Kim. When he graduated from South Oak Cliff High in 1979, he had no plans for his future.

His sisters, though younger, already knew where they were going after high school. Both became All-American basketball players in college. Kim played at Stephen F. Austin State University in Nacogdoches, Texas. Debra was a member of a national championship team at Louisiana Tech. She later played a year with the Dallas Diamonds of the Women's Professional Basketball League and five more years of basketball in Europe.

Meanwhile, Dennis was hanging out at video arcades. He was making friends more easily but still showed little responsibility. He started hanging out with a bad crowd—and testing his mother's patience.

Shirley Rodman remarried, but Dennis didn't like her new husband. He refused to attend the wedding and seemed pleased when the new marriage fell apart after six months. Soon after, Shirley Rodman's health started to deteriorate. The situation wasn't helped by all the worrying she did over her son.

Then something happened. Dennis Rodman grew. Within two years of finishing high school, he gained eleven inches and now stood six feet eight inches tall. On the one hand, the rapid growth caused him to feel even more gawky and less at ease. But with the height came grace—and a rebirth in the sport of basketball.

Rodman's younger sisters were still looking out for him. A friend of theirs had played basketball at Cooke County Junior

Growing up, Dennis Rodman often played basketball with his sisters. Kim (standing) and Debra (sitting on left) are pictured here with their mother, Shirley.

College in Gainesville, Texas. She arranged for a tryout for Dennis in 1982.

A junior college is a two-year college. Many students start in junior college and then move on to a four-year college to complete their studies. Junior colleges are sometimes a good starting place for people who struggled through high school. For athletes, as well, junior colleges provide an opportunity to develop their skills before going on to a larger four-year school.

The coaches at Cooke County Junior College were excited about Dennis Rodman. Never mind that he had never played organized basketball. He was a six-foot-eight-inch African-American kid who had grown up in the big city. That was enough for him to receive a two-year scholarship.

For the first time, he would also be living away from home. Gainesville is approximately seventy miles north of Dallas. In some ways, it was a good situation for Rodman. He felt at ease, living on his own at a small college.

He also performed well as the starting center on the Cooke County basketball team. Rodman was averaging more than 17 points a game and bringing down an average of 16 rebounds per game. But it all screeched to a halt after sixteen games. The one place Dennis Rodman wasn't getting the job done was in the classroom. He had little confidence in his ability to do school work and never really gave it a try. As a result, he flunked out of school. He had blown his chance at playing basketball—and more importantly—at getting an education.

He moved back with his mother in Dallas and started drifting again. By this time, his mother had run out of patience. She figured she wasn't doing her son any favors by letting him stay at home—with no ambition. She told him to get out on his own and do something with his life. Dennis Rodman stayed with friends but still did not seem to be on the road to anything worthwhile.

Rodman is shown here with his mother around the time he left home to play basketball for Cooke County Junior College.

Shirley Rodman said:

> I knew where he was at all times, and it was very tough
> not to give in and let him come back home. I told him he
> had three choices: get a good job, go into the military
> service, or go to school. I would support him in any of
> those things.

Fortunately for Rodman, his time at Cooke County Junior
College had not been a complete waste. While playing there,
he had been spotted by Lonn Reisman, an assistant basketball
coach at Southeastern Oklahoma State University, a four-year
college. Reisman told the team's head coach, Jack Hedden,
about the outstanding center he had watched in Gainesville.
Reisman and Hedden hoped they might be able to recruit
Rodman to play for them when he was done at Cooke County.

By the time they checked back, however, Rodman was no
longer at the junior college. It took some detective work on
the part of the coaches, but eventually Hedden and Reisman
tracked him down in Dallas.

They spoke to Rodman's mother first. She saw this as
another opportunity for her son—perhaps his last. Between
Shirley Rodman and the Southeastern Oklahoma State
coaches, they convinced Dennis to give college another shot.

Rodman also sensed the importance of the chance before
him. As he left for Oklahoma, he made a promise to himself:
"I will never come back to Dallas until I have made something
of my life."

Chapter 3

Dennis Rodman was determined but still lacking in confidence when he arrived at the Southeastern Oklahoma campus in Durant in the middle of 1983.

Meanwhile, in a small town named Bokchito, fifteen miles from Durant, there was a boy, eight years younger than Rodman, who was dealing with his own trauma.

Bryne Rich had been out hunting with friends the previous Halloween. His shotgun accidentally discharged, and his best friend, Brad Robinson, was shot in the chest. Brad died a few days later. Even though everyone realized it was an accident, Bryne was terribly upset. He couldn't sleep at night, and his parents were worried sick about him.

The following year the Riches sent their son to a basketball camp at Southeastern Oklahoma State, hoping this would be something to excite him and get him out of his funk.

What excited him was the counselor assigned to his group. Rich came home each night and told his parents about the counselor named Worm whom he had met. By the end of the

Soon after they got to know one another, Bryne Rich told Dennis Rodman about the tragedy with Brad and said he didn't even want to go on living after his best friend had died. Rodman told him, "That means you have to live twice as hard. You have to live for Brad, too."

Bryne Rich agreed, but pointed out that Dennis Rodman wasn't trying too hard with his life. Rodman thought for a moment and said, "I will if you will."

It was a deal that worked out well for both young men. Bryne Rich was able to get over the past and was much happier. Dennis Rodman found stability with the Riches. He had a dorm room on campus back in Durant. But he spent a great deal of time with the Rich family, often staying overnight at their house.

Back in Dallas, Shirley Rodman was happy her son had found someone to look over him. "My daughters had 'campus parents' when they went off to school. I was relieved Dennis had also found this sort of thing."

Dennis Rodman did well at Southeastern Oklahoma, both as a student and as an athlete. He became an extremely popular person both on campus and in the community.

Sometimes small towns such as Durant have an image of not being tolerant of African Americans. But the school's athletic director, Don Parham, says the African Americans who came to Southeastern Oklahoma fit right in. "For these athletes, Durant is a much calmer place than the cities they came from."

As far as basketball goes, Parham remembers the hustle and spirit Dennis Rodman brought to the team. "He was always diving after loose balls, beating everyone down the court on a fast break, and making slam dunks."

Rodman was also learning about the other part of the game—defense. Coaches Hedden and Reisman helped him

It pleased Rodman's mother to know that the Riches were looking after her son while he was in Oklahoma.

develop the great defensive skills that would make him a star in the NBA. They also worked with him on rebounding.

Pulling down missed shots—both those of others and his own—became a great joy to him. But the coaches weren't done with their lesson yet. They talked to Rodman about another type of rebounding. They taught him that rebounding—coming back from tough breaks or trouble—was an even more important skill in life than in basketball.

Dennis Rodman proved to be an able rebounder, on and off the court.

He was nervous as he rode the team bus north from Durant for his first game with the Southeastern Oklahoma State Savages. "I hope I don't let you down tonight," he said to Reisman. The assistant coach had confidence in his new player; by the end of the night, Rodman was starting to develop some as well.

Rodman had a fine first half against Langston University. But it was what he did in the closing minute that was spectacular. The Savages clung to a three-point lead and were attempting to stall. But when Rodman got the ball, he put it on the floor and started dribbling toward the basket. He took two huge steps, then leaped in the air, and finished the play with a tremendous dunk. Southeastern Oklahoma held on to win the game. Rodman ended up with 24 points and 19 rebounds.

The next game was against Austin College in Sherman, Texas. The Rich family was able to attend this game, although they didn't arrive until the second half. Rodman responded to their presence by scoring 25 points to finish with a game total of 40. After the game, Coach Hedden gave Rodman permission to have Bryne Rich ride back with the team on the bus.

From then on, Bryne Rich attended most of the Savages' games. Most were played within a few hours of Durant. The home games were at the Bloomer Sullivan Gym, named after a former coach at the school. The gym was better known as the "Snake Pit." It seemed like a fitting name to opponents because the Savages were nearly unbeatable at home.

In 1983–84, though, the Savages were hard to beat anywhere. The players thought Bryne Rich was bringing them luck by being at their games. As a result, they made him the team's water boy. Now he had an official position with the team and was with them constantly. The other players called him "Little Worm."

As for Dennis Rodman, he quickly emerged as a team leader. It wasn't just his outstanding play. The other team members looked up to him, even though he was just a sophomore.

Parham remembers how Rodman could keep his composure, even in battles under the backboards:

> In college, where they allow zone defenses, a great center like Dennis is going to get roughed up a lot under the basket. He took his share of shots but he never retaliated. I never saw Dennis take a cheap shot at anyone even though he took a few from others.

The Savages finished the regular season with an 18–9 record. They would now play in the District 9 playoffs for a chance to advance to the thirty-two-team NAIA (small college) national championship tournament in Kansas City.

Southeastern Oklahoma won its first three games. In one of them, against Weatherford College, Rodman had 42 points and 24 rebounds. They were one game away from the national tournament when they were finally stopped.

It was a great season, but Dennis Rodman took the final loss hard. Some of the disappointment was eased a few weeks later when he learned he had been named to the NAIA All-American team.

The next season was even better—both for the Savages and Dennis Rodman. They won 20 games during the regular season, the final win coming against Bethany Nazarene College in the Snake Pit. It was another good game for Dennis Rodman as he tallied 39 points and pulled down 27 rebounds.

The same two teams met in the first game of the District 9 playoffs. The Savages won again as Rodman scored 51 points. This time Southeastern Oklahoma made it through the district playoffs to advance to the national tournament. They won their first two games to advance to the quarterfinals before they were knocked out. Dennis Rodman was the nation's top rebounder and, once again, was named to the All-American team. For the first time, Rodman thought that he'd make it in the pros.

In Rodman's senior season, the Savages closed the regular season with 16 consecutive wins. They made it 19 in a row by breezing through the district playoffs, earning another spot in the national tournament. They won their first three games, the final one by three points over Southwest Texas. Rodman had 15 rebounds in that game. The biggest one was his last. The Savages were protecting a one-point lead as Southwest Texas put up a shot that was no good. A number of players went up for the rebound, but no one soared higher than Rodman. He came down with it, helping preserve the victory that put his team in the Final Four.

In the semi-final game, they lost to the University of Arkansas at Monticello. It was a heartbreaking loss. Though deeply disappointed, Rodman was in top form for the third-place game against St. Thomas Aquinas of New York. It would be his last college game, and he decided to go out in a big way. He scored 46 points and had an incredible 32 rebounds as the Savages won, 75–74.

For the second straight year, Dennis Rodman finished the season as the nation's leading rebounder, averaging 17.8 per game.

Although Southeastern Oklahoma did not win the national championship, Rodman was named to the NAIA All-American team. Here, Rodman accepts the award with Southeastern Oklahoma coach Jack Hedden by his side.

He knew he wouldn't be one of the most sought-after players leaving college that year. But Rodman hoped he would at least be drafted by an NBA team. *Sport* magazine, in analyzing the college crop of players, called Rodman "an active athlete around the hoop who runs the floor like a gazelle and wants the NBA dream in the worst way."

On the day of the NBA draft, Rodman went to the Riches' house. Finally, he got the news: He had been drafted in the second round by the Detroit Pistons. The house erupted in cheers. Dennis Rodman felt overwhelmed, but Bryne Rich was hardly surprised.

"I told you!" he shouted. "I knew you'd make it!"

Chapter 4

The Pistons were an up-and-coming team when Dennis Rodman joined them in 1986. They had been the NBA doormat just a few seasons before. Isiah Thomas, fresh out of Indiana University, joined the team in 1981 and soon became one of the top point guards in the league. Two years later, Chuck Daly took over as head coach, and the Pistons made the playoffs for the first time in seven years.

The Pistons were 46–36 the year before Dennis Rodman joined them and had been knocked out of the playoffs in the first round. They hoped Dennis Rodman and John Salley, their first-round draft pick, could help them advance further in the playoffs this time around.

Rodman saw limited playing time his first year but still made contributions. He could play at several different positions, but power forward was his strongest. Detroit won 52 games in 1986–87 to finish second in the Central Division, five games behind the Atlanta Hawks.

But they beat the Hawks in the playoffs and advanced all the way to the Eastern Conference finals before losing a heartbreaking series to the Boston Celtics. It was after this series that Rodman made his controversial comments about Larry Bird being overrated. Many people were angered by his comments but Rodman also had some supporters. One was his father, Phil, who sent Dennis a letter of encouragement. This was the first communication between the two in years.

Rodman saw much more playing time his second season in the league. He even scored 11.6 points per game, the only time in his career he averaged in double figures in scoring. Chuck Daly, in addition to being an outstanding coach, was a superb teacher. He helped Rodman greatly in his development as a player.

Although he normally didn't start, Rodman was often the Pistons' first substitute to enter the game. In basketball, perhaps more than any other sport, this role is seen as extremely important. In fact, the NBA even has a Sixth Man Award to recognize the best substitute in the league.

Rodman frequently entered the game when defense was needed. Although he had been a tremendous scorer in college, he now made his contributions in other parts of the game.

The Pistons finished first in the the Central Division in 1988 and made it back to the conference finals. Once again, they played the Boston Celtics. This time, the Pistons were victorious. Rodman had the task of guarding Larry Bird. He was able to hold the Boston star to 19 points per game, 10 points below Bird's season average.

For the first time since the Pistons had moved to Detroit in 1957, the team would be playing for the NBA championship. Their opponents were the defending champion Los Angeles Lakers, who had great players like Magic Johnson and Kareem Abdul-Jabbar.

The Pistons weren't in awe of these superstars. They gave the Lakers quite a battle. But Los Angeles emerged as the champion again, beating the Pistons, four games to three.

Detroit had made great progress over the past few years. But none of the players, including Rodman, was satisfied yet. They were determined to win it all in 1988–89.

The Pistons had become one of the best defensive teams in the league with Dennis Rodman as their best defense player. He was fitting right in on a team known as the "Bad Boys." It was a roughhouse bunch. Rick Mahorn and center Bill Laimbeer were among the roughest, with Dennis Rodman close behind. Pistons' fans called them aggressive players. Others, who were not Piston fans, called them dirty players.

The Pistons opened the 1988–89 season with eight straight wins. Rodman even moved into the starting lineup as a replacement for forward Adrian Dantley, who broke his jaw in the sixth game of the year. When Dantley returned from the injury, Rodman was back in a reserve role. But, as usual, he was still making contributions.

In December, the Detroit defense—led by Joe Dumars, Vinnie Johnson, and Dennis Rodman—held the Bulls' Michael Jordan to fewer than twenty points in a game for the first time in nearly a year. The next month, Rodman once again had the job of defending Jordan. He kept the Chicago star under control as the Pistons beat the Bulls again.

In February, the Pistons were involved in a trade involving two outstanding forwards. Detroit sent Adrian Dantley to Dallas in exchange for Mark Aguirre. For Rodman, the absence of Dantley meant even more playing time. Coach Daly alternated between Aguirre and Rodman, putting Rodman in when he felt defense was needed.

The Pistons went on to finish the regular season with a record of 63 wins and 19 losses, best in the entire league. This meant they would be ensured the home-court advantage throughout the playoffs.

Along with teammate Joe Dumars, Dennis Rodman was named to the NBA All-Defensive team.

The Pistons opened the playoffs against the Boston Celtics in a three-out-of-five series.

Rodman combined with John Salley to shut down the Celtic offense. Together they blocked seven shots in one quarter and held the Celtics to just ten points in the second period. Rodman had 12 rebounds as the Pistons won by ten.

In game two, Boston opened up a nine-point lead over Detroit in the third quarter. Although the Pistons needed points to close the gap, Coach Daly decided to concentrate on defense. Rodman and Salley entered the game and once again stifled the Celtics. Boston was limited to only 13 points in the final period, and Detroit was able to win the game, 102–95.

The series shifted to Boston for the third game. A win for Detroit would finish off the Celtics. But Boston came alive at home. They scored 55 points in the first half and held a four-point lead late in the third quarter.

They tried to increase it, but a shot missed. Dennis Rodman leaped high and batted at the ball as it bounced off the rim. Finally, he got control of it and started dribbling downcourt. He spun around as he passed the center line and drove toward the basket, jumping in the air as he crossed the free-throw line and stuffing the ball through the basket to pull the Pistons within two points of Boston.

Rodman and Salley turned on the defense in the fourth quarter. They held the Celtics to 12 points the rest of the way and helped the Pistons complete a three-game sweep in the opening playoff series.

Isiah Thomas, the Pistons' great guard, called the Boston series a "showcase for Dennis Rodman." Thomas referred to the incident caused by Rodman's comments about Larry Bird two years before. Then he added:

I'm amazed at how mature the Worm is now. Not only has Dennis developed as a player, as we all knew he would, he has really matured as an individual. Dennis can handle the most difficult of situations now, something that was not easy for him to do when he was a rookie.

In the next round of playoffs, the Pistons swept the Milwaukee Bucks in four straight games. They had now won seven games in a row in the playoffs. Their next series, the Eastern Conference finals against the Chicago Bulls, would not be as easy.

The Bulls took two of the first three. Rodman was hampered by a bad back. Even so, he helped hold Michael Jordan well under his season scoring average in the fourth and fifth games. The Pistons won both to take a 3–2 game lead in the series.

In game six, at Chicago Stadium, the Pistons captured the series with a 103–94 win as Rodman pulled down 15 rebounds. Rodman didn't start any of the playoff games against the Bulls but still had more than 10 rebounds in five of the six games.

The Pistons were Eastern Conference champions again. But they weren't done yet. They would be facing the Los Angeles Lakers for the NBA championship for the second year in a row. This would also mark the end of the career for the Lakers' great center Kareem Abdul-Jabbar, who was retiring at the end of the season.

Rodman's back was still acting up. He sometimes had his back spasms treated right on the bench during the games against the Lakers.

The Pistons opened the championship series at home by beating the Lakers twice. The third game was in Los Angeles, and Rodman came alive. Not only did he have 19 rebounds,

Rodman blocks his longtime opponent Larry Bird in a crucial game against the Boston Celtics.

he also scored 12 points as Detroit won, 114–110. The Pistons were now only one game away from their first-ever NBA championship win.

Dennis Rodman played only twelve minutes in game four, but his time on the floor was memorable. The Lakers opened up an early lead, but Rodman helped keep it from getting bigger as he entered the game in the first quarter.

He slipped between A.C. Green and Kareem Abdul-Jabbar to pull down a missed Laker shot. A few minutes later, at the other end of the court, he again took a rebound away from Abdul-Jabbar and Green. The next time down the floor, however, Rodman pulled up as he felt the muscles in his lower back tighten up. He dropped to his knees in pain as play continued. Finally he got up and hobbled around by the sideline. On the other side of the court, Joe Dumars had the ball. Spotting Rodman open, and not realizing that he was injured, Dumars fired a cross-court pass to him. Even though he was in great pain, Rodman put up a twenty-foot shot that fell through the rim to pull the Pistons within eight points. He held his back and grimaced as he ran back downcourt. Finally play stopped, and he was taken out. He lay on his stomach in front of the bench as the trainer put an ice pack on his back.

Rodman reentered the game in the second half. Detroit continued to whittle at the Laker lead and trailed by only two points after three quarters. In between periods, Rodman told Coach Daly he could continue. He played only the first two minutes of the final quarter but helped shut down the Laker offense long enough for Detroit to take the lead.

Detroit went on to win the game, 105–97. Along with the rest of the Pistons, Dennis Rodman was a world champion.

The team had a chance to celebrate after the game in the locker room. There was an even bigger celebration two days

In the 1988-89 season, Rodman helped the Pistons become the NBA champions. Going into the playoffs with the home-court advantage, the Pistons were able to defeat the mighty Lakers in the finals.

later in Detroit. A huge crowd turned out to cheer the champions, and each player was given a chance to speak.

When it was Dennis Rodman's turn, he started talking about the Riches, his adopted family in Oklahoma. At that point, tears started rolling down his cheeks, and he was unable to continue speaking. Finally, Isiah Thomas stepped up and embraced Rodman as the crowd cheered wildly. It was an emotional time for everyone, especially Dennis Rodman.

The Pistons continued to shine in 1989–90. Isiah Thomas was in his prime, and, with Joe Dumars, the Pistons had one of the league's best backcourts. It was also a notable season for Rodman. For the first time, he earned a spot on the Eastern Conference All-Star team. On top of that, at the end of the season, he was named the NBA's Defensive Player of the Year.

Individual honors were nice. But Dennis Rodman was focused on helping his team win another championship. During the Eastern Conference semifinal series against the New York Knicks, Rodman made one of the biggest plays of the season. The Knicks were trying to tie up the series. New York trailed in the closing minute of the fourth game but took off downcourt on a fast break. Mark Jackson had the ball with a teammate on each side. Jackson glanced both ways, deciding which direction to pass the ball. Had he glanced backwards, he would have seen Dennis Rodman bearing down on him. With long strides, Rodman caught up with Jackson, then reached out and flicked the ball away from him. The fast break was halted, and the Pistons held on to win the game and the series.

There was no stopping them at this point. They returned to the NBA Finals; this time they beat the Portland Trail Blazers for their second consecutive league title.

Although the Pistons' championship streak was halted in 1991, Dennis Rodman was named the Defensive Player of the

Year for the second time in a row. As it turned out, he was just warming up for his best season ever.

Although he had been seen as an important sixth man in the past, Rodman was now even more valuable as a starter. He was seeing more playing time than ever in 1991–92. Eleven times he played an entire game that year, and he became the league's first player in ten years to log more than 3,300 minutes played for the season.

He made the All-Star team again and pulled down 13 rebounds in the All-Star game. For the season, he averaged 18.7 rebounds per game. It was the best rebounding average since Wilt Chamberlain had averaged 19.2 twenty years before. When the season ended, Rodman received the Schick Award, an honor that recognizes all-around contributions by a player to his team.

His greatest game of the year came on March 4, when he had 34 rebounds to set a new team record. After the game he broke into tears as he thought about how far he had come, not just as a player but as a person. Thirty-four rebounds in one game is a tremendous feat. Rodman said, "This is not my greatest achievement. The greatest achievement of my life is turning my life around, fighting off so many things in my life just to get here."

Chapter 5

Dennis Rodman had overcome tough times and emotional hurdles to get where he was. But, as he soon found out, bumps in the road can continue to pop up at any time.

Following the 1991–92 season, Rodman experienced a series of losses. Chuck Daly, a man he respected greatly, stepped down as Pistons' coach. "Daly made me a man," Rodman had once said.

At the same time, his teammate and good friend John Salley left the team as well as the general manager who first signed him to a pro contract, Jack McCloskey.

Also during the off-season, his marriage broke up. Just as devastating, it meant he would rarely see his five-year-old daughter, Alexis. His wife and daughter moved to California, far away from Detroit and Dennis Rodman.

Chuck Daly had once said of Dennis Rodman, "He's a guy who has childlike qualities in a man's body. He wears his emotions on his sleeve and he's so very easy to hurt."

Now Rodman was hurting. He started to withdraw, not wanting to see or talk to anyone. He wouldn't answer his phone or door for quite a while.

Rodman had his family very concerned when he went through a rough time during the 1991-92 season. Here, he is pictured with his sister Debra.

Although he still led the league in rebounding, the 1992–93 season was hard for Rodman. He wasn't comfortable with the new coach, Ron Rothstein, and started missing practices. This was not like him. He was suspended for the missed practices and also missed many other games because of injuries. The Pistons wondered if his injuries were really serious enough to keep him out of so many games. After all, this was a man who had played despite great back pains during the 1989 playoffs. The team thought it was more an attitude problem than physical injuries.

Rodman started drifting back to the aimless existence of his youth. He was no longer the wide-eyed kid who had come into the NBA with so much enthusiasm six years before.

Shirley Rodman said:

> He had so much fun his first few years in the league. And I had such a good time watching him develop. I remember when I would visit him, he was always surrounded by kids. Dennis loved kids. He loved what he was doing when he first started playing with the Pistons. He still has fun with basketball—when they let him.

Dennis Rodman was having very little fun this season, however. In February 1993, Rodman was found sleeping in his truck at five in the morning in the parking lot of the Pistons' arena. There was a loaded rifle under the seat. Rodman admitted being depressed but said he had no intention of harming himself. Even so, Rodman's bizarre behavior was of great concern to those close to him, including the Pistons' organization, which sent him to a psychiatrist.

Despite the problems in his personal life, he was outstanding when he did play. The Pistons, however, couldn't rely on him to be ready to play. For Rodman, the pain continued as the season ended. He disappeared during the summer of 1993. The Pistons had no idea where he was. At one point, Rodman was in Las Vegas.

He was gambling heavily in the casinos and losing large sums of money. Some thought he was losing the money intentionally.

It was something only Rodman could understand—as though he could shed his problems by losing his money and possessions.

Rodman had given away things before. He is a very generous person and often helped homeless people, giving them money and sometimes even taking them home with him. But this wasn't an act of generosity. It was self-destruction, and it had people worried.

To Dennis Rodman, though, it all seemed normal. He's definitely his own man. "If I do something, I can live with it," he once said. "But if society makes me do it, I feel caged."

Dennis Rodman usually doesn't do the types of things society expects. T-shirts and torn jeans are a big part of his wardrobe, even though he can certainly afford much more expensive clothing.

He says he doesn't try to be a role model. "A lot of kids are going to follow what you do, but you're not asking them to do it," he explains. Much of his behavior is the type parents would like their children to follow. For example, Dennis is proud of the fact he doesn't drink, smoke, or take drugs.

But other things about him are hard to figure out. Dennis once said of himself, "I'm a weird person."

But his peculiar behavior had finally gotten to be too much for the Pistons. They loved him, they cared for him, but they no longer wanted to put up with Rodman. Even though the Pistons knew how talented a player Rodman was, they felt they could no longer depend on him.

Shortly before the 1993–94 season opened, the Pistons worked out a trade with the San Antonio Spurs. Along with Isaiah Morris, Rodman was sent to the Spurs in exchange for Sean Elliott and David Wood.

The Pistons wished Rodman well. Most of all, they hoped with his new team he would no longer feel caged.

Chapter 6

The trade to the Spurs was like a new start for Rodman. But there were still signs—visible ones—that he was hurting. He bleached his hair and covered the upper portion of his body with tattoos. To many, this was just Dennis Rodman being himself. "I admire people who don't do what everybody else expects them to do," Rodman said. Dennis Rodman thrives on being different.

Although he was a blond most of the 1993–94 season, he would change hair color if the mood suited him. He played a few games as a redhead, a couple with purple hair, and even hinted that he might dye his hair green on St. Patrick's Day.

As for the tattoos, Dennis says he loves them. "I think it's a way of expressing the way I am inside. I like to show the wildness, the puzzlement of Dennis Rodman. Just when you feel like you've got me figured out, next thing you know, boom! I do something else."

Dennis's trade to San Antonio at least meant he was closer to his mother and sister. The Rodmans were once again in the same state. Debra, after playing basketball in Europe, returned

49

Thinking it best for both the team and Rodman, the Detroit Pistons traded him to the San Antonio Spurs where he would play with the great David Robinson.

to Dallas and got married. She now has a daughter and works for the state of Texas. Kim has two daughters and does accounting for a moving company. She also lives in Dallas.

As for Rodman's mom, she is an office administrator for a plywood and door company. She still volunteers at her church but finally gave up teaching voice and playing music at the church as actual jobs.

Rodman has a house in San Antonio and an apartment in Dallas. This allows him to spend time with his family as well as keep an eye out on a business he started a few years ago. He is part-owner of an earth-moving company, Rodman Excavating, in Frisco, Texas.

He wants to help his mother, just as she helped him while he struggled growing up. But Rodman's offers of help are sometimes a source of disagreement between the two. "He wants me to quit my job and let him support me," Shirley Rodman said.

As an independent person, Shirley remembers how difficult it was to get Dennis to quit depending on her years earlier. She fears that quitting her job would allow the opposite situation to happen. "You lose your identity when you do that. I like having a reason to get up in the morning."

Rodman's new coach in San Antonio was John Lucas, a man who had also dealt with and overcome troubles. Because of his past, Lucas seemed well equipped to understand Dennis Rodman and his strange ways. "Dennis had a problem and dealt with it the wrong way," said Lucas. "I did the same thing . . ."

The Spurs didn't question Rodman's talent. They felt they needed help rebounding. Most of the burden had fallen on their star center, David Robinson. The Spurs hoped Rodman could give some relief to Robinson in his rebounding duties. The team also looked forward to the added defense Rodman could provide.

The addition of Rodman to the San Antonio Spurs took the burden of rebounding off center David Robinson's shoulders.

Rodman especially impressed the Spurs with his basketball knowledge, the work he did to study the game, and the players he played well against.

"He has the highest basketball IQ of anyone I've ever talked to," said San Antonio vice president Bob Bass. "We knew he could rebound and play defense. What we didn't realize was how well he passes and sets screens, how aware he is on the court."

Lucas looked to Dennis Rodman to become one of the team's leaders, a coach of sorts on the floor.

Some people found it odd for Rodman to assume the role of leader. The media criticized Rodman for his sometimes curious behavior. He had many strange habits, including taking off his shoes and not paying attention during time-outs.

But Lucas and the other coaches would not concern themselves with such things. "Here's a guy who gets you 18 rebounds a game, shuts down the other team's top scorer, frees your scorers up, and sets hard screens," said Spurs' assistant coach Tom Thibodeau. "We judge him by what he does between the lines."

Soon after they acquired Rodman from the Pistons, Lucas told the rest of the players on the team, "Dennis does things a little bit different from other guys. Does anyone have a problem with that?" No one did.

Rodman got off to a good start with his new team, pulling down 21 rebounds in the season opener. He fit in well with the Spurs' star, David Robinson.

Robinson admitted he had his doubts about Rodman when the team traded for him:

> I didn't know anything about Dennis except what I read, and none of that was positive. Then when I met him and saw he was interested only in playing hard and winning, that he was happy to play with us, that kind of eased my

concern. Dennis adds a lot of toughness and offensive rebounding. It takes a lot of pressure off me.

Others agreed that Rodman's presence in the Spurs' lineup was helping Robinson. To many, the mark of a great player is his ability to make his teammates better. During the year, Rodman was often credited with elevating Robinson's game. One of the comments came from an opposing coach, Mike Dunleavy of the Milwaukee Bucks:

Rodman has helped David's intensity. He doesn't have the rebounding load on his shoulders night in and night out, but he does have the competitiveness with Rodman to get his numbers on the board, too.

Flanked by Rodman, Robinson went on to the greatest season of his career. He won the league's scoring championship for the first time and finished second in the balloting for the NBA's Most Valuable Player award.

Rodman was, as usual, content to let others get the points. He even told Lucas not to design a single offense play for him, saying it didn't matter if he shot the ball all season.

"He's the only player I've ever seen who just doesn't care about offense," said teammate Antoine Carr. "He really doesn't care if he takes any shots or not.

"I've played with a lot of players, but I've never seen anyone like him."

Rodman saw himself as filling a different role on the team than David Robinson. And this referred to more than just scoring or not scoring points. Dennis still had the bad boy image from his years with the Pistons while Robinson had a more clean-cut image. "I'm going to be the bad guy," said Dennis, "and Dave's going to be the good guy, going to church and doing all the right things." Such an arrangement was fine with both Robinson and Rodman.

Truly a team player, Rodman takes charge on the court. He does all he can to ensure that his team will win—never worrying about grabbing the spotlight by scoring points.

"We get along extremely well," said Robinson. "Our relationship is mainly based on the respect we have for each other on the floor."

The previous year, the Spurs had fallen apart in the second half of the season and finished six games behind the Houston Rockets in the Midwest Division. In mid-January of 1994, they had a brief slump that dropped them to third place. They hoped to stop the skid before it got any worse.

In their next game, the Spurs were on fire in a game against the Dallas Mavericks. Rodman had 20 rebounds in the first half alone. He finished the game with 32. Although it was two shy of his career best, his performance did set a Spurs' record. He now held the team rebounding record for two different clubs. The Spurs beat the Mavericks by twenty points. It would be more than a month before they would lose again.

Both Rodman and David Robinson were magnificent during the Spurs' thirteen-game winning streak. As usual, Robinson received most of the attention. Meanwhile, Rodman was averaging more than 19 rebounds per game during the amazing streak.

Through it all, he continued to shoot very little. In the game following his 32-rebound performance, he had 20 rebounds and no points. Three weeks before that, he had a game in which he scored only 2 points but had 23 rebounds.

As he had done with the Pistons, Rodman made numerous contributions without scoring. He led the league in rebounding most of the year and finished the season with 17.3 rebounds per game, far ahead of Shaquille O'Neal of the Orlando Magic, who finished second. It was the third consecutive year that Rodman had been the NBA's leading rebounder. In addition, he helped the Spurs become one of the league's top defensive teams. He effectively guarded some of the NBA's top scorers, including Shawn Kemp of the Seattle

During the Spurs thirteen-game winning streak, Rodman averaged more than 19 rebounds per game.

Supersonics, Charles Barkley of the Phoenix Suns, and Hakeem Olajuwon of the Houston Rockets.

The Spurs competed all season with the Rockets for first place in the Midwest Division. It was Hakeem Olajuwon, the Rockets' outstanding center, who ended up edging out Robinson as the league's Most Valuable Player in 1993–94.

But while the centers got the headlines, Rodman continued with his behind-the-scenes work. The attention he did receive in the press usually centered around his behavior. His hard style of play was regarded by some as being too rough. Dennis says of his critics, "They want to put diapers on us. But that's not the way I play. When I step on the court, I play mean. Forget all that nice stuff."

But not everyone was forgetting this. Dennis received more than his share of technical fouls and flagrant fouls. Often he reacted to these calls strongly. During a time he was wearing a protective face mask, he sometimes ripped the mask off and slammed it to the floor. Once he stripped off his jersey. On another occasion, he was ejected from a game because of an outburst. He refused to leave the court and instead, flung an equipment bag onto the floor.

Rodman's behavior reached the point that Commissioner David Stern of the NBA ordered him to tone down his antics. Coach Lucas also let Rodman know he didn't approve of some of the things he did. But Lucas was careful not to cramp Rodman's style or his personality to the point that it would make him a less effective player.

"Nobody's asking him to sell out," said Lucas. "The only thing I ask for is that there be no repercussions that could cost us the next game."

The Spurs ended up with a 55–27 record, three games behind the Rockets. They still made the playoffs and faced the Utah Jazz in the opening round.

Rodman had 11 rebounds in the first game of the series as the Spurs won, 106–89.

In the second game, though, both the Spurs and Dennis Rodman fell apart. Utah beat San Antonio by 12 points to even the series at one game apiece. For Rodman, things were even worse. His performance was fine (17 rebounds and 14 points). It was the way he played that drew criticism.

At one point, he undercut the Jazz's Tom Chambers as he went up for a basket. Later, as Utah guard John Stockton ran by, Dennis kneed him in the thigh.

Not only was Rodman ejected from the game, he was fined $10,000 and handed a one-game suspension, causing him to miss the next game. Without Rodman, the Spurs lost game three by thirty-three points. Two nights later, Rodman was back, but Utah won again to knock San Antonio out of the playoffs.

Getting eliminated in the opening round was disappointing to the San Antonio press, players, and fans. All had expected more. Some blamed Rodman for the loss.

The season, for Rodman, ended on a low note. He had a good relationship with his coach, but that ended the next month when John Lucas left the team. Lucas ended up as the coach of the Philadelphia 76ers. The Spurs eventually signed Bob Hill as coach for the 1994–95 season.

Two years before, Rodman had trouble dealing with the departure of Chuck Daly as coach of the Pistons. Now another coach he regarded highly had left.

As he had before, Rodman had difficulty dealing with the change. During the 1994 preseason, he did not react well to the strict rules of his new coach. He arrived late for one exhibition and was ejected from another after arguing with an official.

As a result, the Spurs suspended Rodman and started the season without him. Once again, Rodman was facing personal and professional problems.

Rodman finally played his first game more than a month into the season. He got a warm response from the fans as he entered the Spurs' game against the Washington Bullets on December 13. Soon, he was back in the starting lineup, and the Spurs were happy to have him. They had lost nine of their first sixteen games without him. After his return, though, the Spurs quickly established themselves as the best team in the NBA.

Even with the late start, Rodman went on to lead the league in rebounding for the fourth-straight time. The Spurs finished the regular season with 62 wins and 20 losses, the best record in the league. They were aiming for the NBA championship and would be satisfied with nothing less.

Unfortunately, things didn't work out for Rodman and the Spurs. They beat Denver and Los Angeles in the opening playoff rounds, but lost to the Houston Rockets in the conference finals.

On October 2, 1995 Dennis Rodman was traded to the Chicago Bulls in exchange for reserve center Will Perdue and other unnamed considerations. The Bulls did not re-sign guard Pete Myers or forward Larry Krystowiak in order to make room for Rodman under the salary cap.

Rodman joined a Bulls team featuring All-Stars Michael Jordan and Scottie Pippen. With the departure of Horace Grant, he filled Chicago's need for a rebounding forward. He helped the Bulls win the NBA championship for the 1995–96 season.

With Rodman, Jordan, and Pippen returning for the 1996–97 NBA season, the Bulls breezed through another regular season. Although Rodman suffered from injuries throughout the campaign, limiting him to only 55 games, he was still one of the top rebounders in the league. His skill of grabbing boards helped the Bulls win another World

Championship. This title was Rodman's fifth in his eleventh season.

Although there had been talk of breaking up the Bulls' nucleus of Jordan, Pippen, and Rodman after the 1996–97 campaign, they returned for one last run at the NBA title the following season. Rodman continued to dominate the boards, averaging 15.0 rebounds per game to capture his seventh consecutive rebounding title. Chicago won its sixth title in eight years by defeating the Utah Jazz in the NBA Finals in six games.

The Bulls' dynasty came to an end, as Jordan retired and Pippen was traded to the Houston Rockets. Rodman retired briefly then signed with the struggling Los Angeles Lakers on February 23, 1999. He made quite an impact, leading the Lakers to ten straight wins immediately after he was signed. However, his antics quickly became a distraction and he was released.

It was unclear whether Rodman would sign with any team just prior to the 1999–2000 campaign.

Career Statistics

Year	G	Min.	FGM	FGA	Pct.	FTM	FTA	Pct.	Reb.	Pts.	Reb. Avg.	Pts. Avg.
1986–87	77	1,155	213	391	.545	74	126	.587	332	500	4.3	6.5
1987–88	82	2,147	398	709	.561	152	284	.535	715	953	8.7	11.6
1988–89	82	2,208	316	531	.595	97	155	.626	772	735	9.4	9.0
1989–90	82	2,377	288	496	.581	142	217	.654	792	719	9.7	8.8
1990–91	82	2,747	276	560	.493	111	176	.631	1,026	669	12.5	8.2
1991–92	82	3,301	342	635	.539	84	140	.600	1,530	800	18.6	9.8
1992–93	62	2,410	183	429	.427	87	163	.534	1,132	468	18.3	7.5
1993–94	79	2,989	156	292	.534	53	102	.520	1,367	370	17.3	4.7
1994–95	49	1,568	137	240	.571	75	111	.676	823	349	16.8	7.1
1995–96	64	2,088	146	304	.480	56	106	.528	952	351	14.9	5.5
1996–97	55	1,947	128	286	.448	50	88	.568	883	311	16.1	5.7
1997–98	80	2,856	155	360	.431	61	111	.550	1,201	375	15.0	4.7
1998–99	23	657	16	46	.348	17	39	.436	258	49	11.2	2.1
TOTALS	899	28,450	2,754	5,279	.522	1,059	1,818	.583	11,783	6,649	13.1	7.4

G—Games Played
Min.—Minutes Played
FGM—Field Goals Made
FGA—Field Goals Attempted

FTM—Free Throws Made
FTA—Free Throws Attempted
Reb.—Rebounds
Pts.—Points Scored

Where to Write Dennis Rodman:

Mr. Dennis Rodman
NBA Players Association
1700 Broadway, Suite 1400
New York, NY 10019

On the Internet at: http://www.nba.com/players

Index